The Perfect Gown

Level 6 – Orange

Helpful Hints for Reading at Home

The graphemes (written letters) and phonemes (units of sound) used throughout this series are aligned with Letters and Sounds. This offers a consistent approach to learning, whether reading at home or in the classroom.

HERE IS A LIST OF GRAPHEMES FOR THIS PHASE OF LEARNING. AN EXAMPLE OF THE PRONUNCIATION CAN BE FOUND IN BRACKETS.

Phase 5			
ay (day)	ou (out)	ie (tie)	ea (eat)
oy (boy)	ir (girl)	ue (blue)	aw (saw)
wh (when)	ph (photo)	ew (new)	oe (toe)
au (Paul)	a_e (make)	e_e (these)	i_e (like)
o_e (home)	u_e (rule)		

Phase 5 Alternative Pronunciations of Graphemes			
a (hat, what)	e (bed, she)	i (fin, find)	o (hot, so, other)
u (but, unit)	c (cat, cent)	g (got, giant)	ow (cow, blow)
ie (tied, field)	ea (eat, bread)	er (farmer, herb)	ch (chin, school, chef)
y (yes, by, very)	ou (out, shoulder, could, you)		

HERE ARE SOME WORDS WHICH YOUR CHILD MAY FIND TRICKY.

Phase 5 Tricky Words			
oh	their	people	Mr
Mrs	looked	called	asked
could			

TOP TIPS FOR HELPING YOUR CHILD TO READ:

- Allow children time to break down unfamiliar words into units of sound and then encourage children to string these sounds together to create the word.

- Encourage your child to point out any focus phonics when they are used.

- Read through the book more than once to grow confidence.

- Ask simple questions about the text to assess understanding.

- Encourage children to use illustrations as prompts.

This book focuses on /ir/ and /u_e/ and is an Orange level 6 book band.

The Perfect Gown

Written by
Shalini Vallepur

Illustrated by
Emily Cowling

Perfect Pamela jumped out of bed. She was so happy. "It's my birthday next week, and I need the perfect gown!"

Perfect Pamela put on her perfect crown. She needed all the people around her to help her have the perfect gown for her birthday.

Perfect Pamela's dad was the king, and she was the most spoilt person in all of the land. People had to bow down to Perfect Pamela when she entered the room.

"It's my birthday next week! All of you must help me get the perfect gown. Do not disappoint me!" Perfect Pamela said.

First, Perfect Pamela went to her maids. "Bring me the best gowns you have!" she shouted.

The maids rushed to bring the best gown for Perfect Pamela. They hoped they were not going to disappoint her.

"I look like a clown!" Perfect Pamela said with a scowl. Her maids had given her a gown that had lots of frills and big red clown boots. Her face had been powdered, too.

"Take this cash and go to town! Get me the perfect gown, now!" Perfect Pamela yelled at her maids.

The rude girl went to see the cooks.
"I want the best cake for my birthday! It had better be moist, or you will be punished" she yelled.

The cooks were frightened of Perfect Pamela. They started mixing up a cake and getting small, sweet flowers to put on top.

The maids came back home. They bowed down to Perfect Pamela..

"This was the last gown left at the dress shop," said one of the maids.
"I hope it does not disappoint you," said a different maid..

Perfect Pamela put the dress on. She hated it! It was brown and ripped, and it smelt like mud and dirt.

Perfect Pamela was boiling with rage. The gown was horrid and smelt a bit! She threw her crown down in a huff.

"You are all spoiling my birthday!" Perfect Pamela yelled in a rude way.
"I do not want a rubbish, brown gown!"

"What's all this fuss?" said the King, who was looking a bit annoyed..

"Pappa! The maids are spoiling my birthday with this horrid gown!" said Perfect Pamela. The maids looked upset.

"Perfect Pamela! These maids and all the people around you are toiling over this birthday!" said the King. "If you cannot be good, then you will have no gown at all!"

Perfect Pamela stormed away. She went and sat on the mud with the cows and pigs in the farmyard.

"Pappa was so upset with me, but I need the perfect gown! I cannot go to my birthday party without one," said Perfect Pamela, looking sad.

"Oink," said the pig.

"But Pappa is right, people are toiling night and day to get me the perfect gown. I must make it up to them," she said.

Perfect Pamela went to see the cooks. "Do not bow to me, I was such a spoilt girl."
"We forgive you," said the cooks.

Then Perfect Pamela went to see the maids. "I have been so rude. Please join me for my birthday party, I do not need a gown or a crown!"

"Thank you, Perfect Pamela," said the maids.
"We just wish for you to be pleased."

Perfect Pamela woke up on her birthday to a big surprise. A gown was waiting for her. It was the same shade as a pink rose. It was perfect.

She ran downstairs and there was a fantastic birthday cake with cute flowers on top. Perfect Pamela had a great birthday!

The Perfect Gown

1. Why does Perfect Pamela need the perfect gown?

2. How can you tell that Perfect Pamela is being rude to her maids?

3. What type of dress did the maids bring back from the town?
   - (a) A brown and ripped dress
   - (b) A beautiful pink dress
   - (c) A dress that was too small for Perfect Pamela

4. What did Perfect Pamela find waiting for her on her birthday?

5. Do you think Perfect Pamela was right to say sorry? What would you have done if you were one of Perfect Pamela's maids or cooks?

© This edition published in 2023. First published in 2020.
BookLife Publishing Ltd.
King's Lynn, Norfolk, PE30 4LS, UK

ISBN 978-1-80505-001-8

All rights reserved. Printed in Poland.
A catalogue record for this book is
available from the British Library.

The Perfect Gown
Written by Shalini Vallepur
Illustrated by Emily Cowling

An Introduction to BookLife Readers...

Our Readers have been specifically created in line with the London Institute of Education's approach to book banding and are phonetically decodable and ordered to support each phase of the Letters and Sounds document.

Each book has been created to provide the best possible reading and learning experience. Our aim is to share our love of books with children, providing both emerging readers and prolific page-turners with beautiful books that are guaranteed to provoke interest and learning, regardless of ability.

BOOK BAND GRADED using the Institute of Education's approach to levelling.

PHONETICALLY DECODABLE supporting each phase of Letters and Sounds.

EXERCISES AND QUESTIONS to offer reinforcement and to ascertain comprehension.

BEAUTIFULLY ILLUSTRATED to inspire and provoke engagement, providing a variety of styles for the reader to enjoy whilst reading through the series.

AUTHOR INSIGHT:
SHALINI VALLEPUR

Passionate about books from a very young age, Shalini Vallepur received the award of Norfolk County Scholar for her outstanding grades. Later on she read English at the University of Leicester, where she stayed to complete her Modern Literature MA. Whilst at university, Shalini volunteered as a Storyteller to help children learn to read, which gave her experience and expertise in the way children pick up and retain information. She used her knowledge and her background and implemented them in the 32 books that she has written for BookLife Publishing. Shalini's writing easily takes us to different worlds, and the serenity and quality of her words are sure to captivate any child who picks up her books.

This book focuses on /ir/ and /u_e/ and is an Orange level 6 book band.